MW01225476

KS2
9–10
Years

Master Maths at Home

Geometry and Shape

Scan the QR code to help
your child's learning at home.

How to use this book

Maths — No Problem! created **Master Maths at Home** to help children develop fluency in the subject and a rich understanding of core concepts.

Key features of the Master Maths at Home books include:

- Carefully designed lessons that provide structure, but also allow flexibility in how they're used.

- Speech bubbles containing content designed to spark diverse conversations, with many discussion points that don't have obvious 'right' or 'wrong' answers.

- Rich illustrations that will guide children to a discussion of shapes and units of measurement, allowing them to make connections to the wider world around them.

- Exercises that allow a flexible approach and can be adapted to suit any child's cognitive or functional ability.

- Clearly laid-out pages that encourage children to practise a range of higher-order skills.

- A community of friendly and relatable characters who introduce each lesson and come along as your child progresses through the series.

You can see more guidance on how to use these books at **mastermathsathome.com**.

We're excited to share all the ways you can learn maths!

Copyright © 2022 Maths — No Problem!

Maths — No Problem!
mastermathsathome.com
www.mathsnoproblem.com
hello@mathsnoproblem.com

First published in Great Britain in 2022 by
Dorling Kindersley Limited
One Embassy Gardens, 8 Viaduct Gardens, London SW11 7BW
A Penguin Random House Company

The authorised representative in the EEA is Dorling Kindersley
Verlag GmbH. Arnulfstr. 124, 80636 Munich, Germany

10 9 8 7 6 5 4 3 2 1
001–327100–May/22

All rights reserved. Without limiting the rights under the copyright reserved above, no part of this publication may be reproduced, stored in, or introduced into a retrieval system, or transmitted, in any form, or by any means (electronic, mechanical, photocopying, recording, or otherwise), without the prior written permission of the copyright owner.

A CIP catalogue record for this book is available from the British Library.

ISBN: 978-0-24153-945-3
Printed and bound in the UK

For the curious
www.dk.com

This book was made with Forest Stewardship Council™ certified paper – one small step in DK's commitment to a sustainable future. For more information go to www.dk.com/our-green-pledge

Acknowledgements

The publisher would like to thank the authors and consultants Andy Psarianos, Judy Hornigold, Adam Gifford and Dr Anne Hermanson.

The Castledown typeface has been used with permission from the Colophon Foundry.

Contents

Ruby   Elliott   Amira   Charles   Lulu   Sam   Oak   Holly   Ravi   Emma   Jacob   Hannah

Properties of angles

Starter

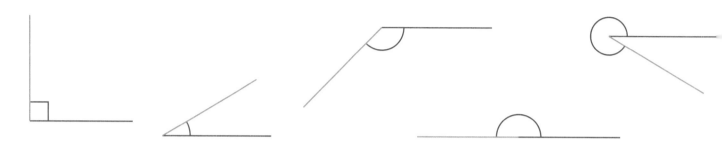

How can we describe these angles?

Example

The two lines that form this angle are perpendicular. This is a **right angle**.

We can identify a right angle with this symbol.

This angle is less than a right angle. This is an **acute angle**.

This angle is more than a right angle. This is an **obtuse angle**.

This is 2 right angles. It is a **straight angle**.

This angle is more than a straight angle or 2 right angles. This is a **reflex angle**.

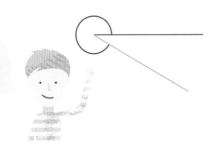

Practice

1 Fill in the blanks.

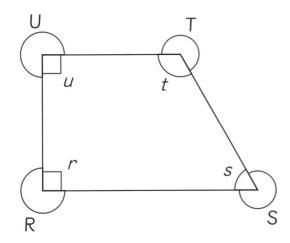

(a) Angle *u* is a _____ angle.

(b) Angle U is a _____ angle.

(c) Angle _____ is an obtuse angle.

(d) Angle *s* is an _____ angle.

(e) There are _____ reflex angles. (f) There are _____ right angles.

2 Use the space to draw some triangles to help you answer the questions.

(a) The interior of a triangle can have up to:

_____ acute angle(s)

_____ right angle(s)

_____ obtuse angle(s)

Angles inside a shape are called **interior angles**.

(b) The interior of a triangle must have at least 2 _____ angles.

Measuring angles

Starter

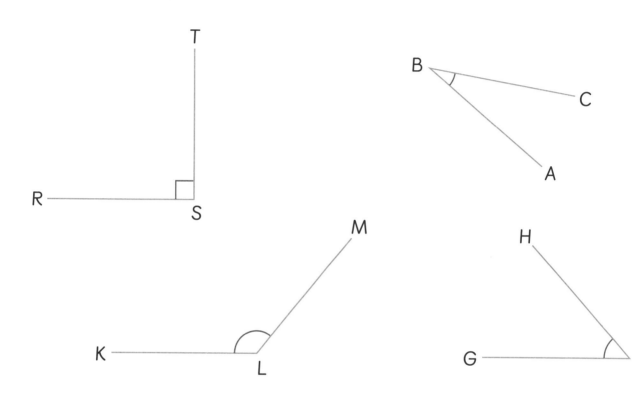

How can we measure these angles?

Example

We use a protractor to measure angles.

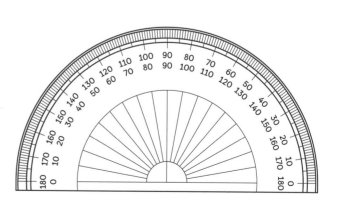

We measure angles in degrees.

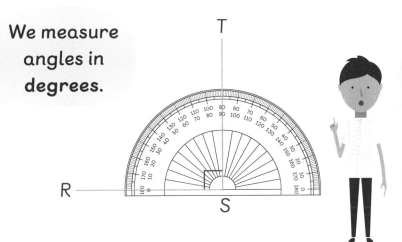

∠RST is 90 degrees. We write 90 degrees as **90°**.

∠RST is a right angle. All right angles are 90°.

We need to align the vertex to the origin of the protractor.

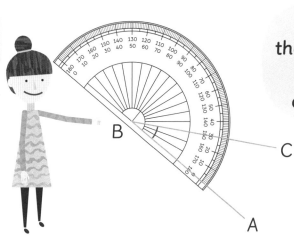

∠CBA is less than a right angle. It is an acute angle. It is 30°.

∠HFG is also an acute angle. It is 48°.

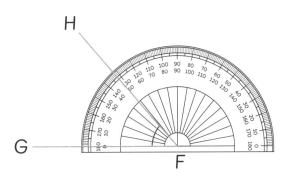

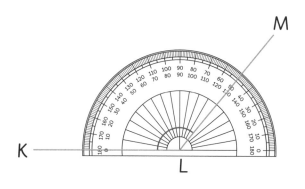

∠KLM is more than 90°, so it is an obtuse angle.

We measure angles in degrees using a protractor.

∠RST = 90°   ∠CBA = 30°   ∠HFG = 48°   ∠KLM = 130°

Use a protractor to measure each angle.
Fill in the blanks and circle the correct word to describe the angle.

1 P

∠PQR = ☐ °

∠PQR is (acute / obtuse / right / straight).

R

Q

2

∠ZYX = ☐ °

Z

X ——————————————— Y

∠ZYX is (acute / obtuse / right / straight).

B

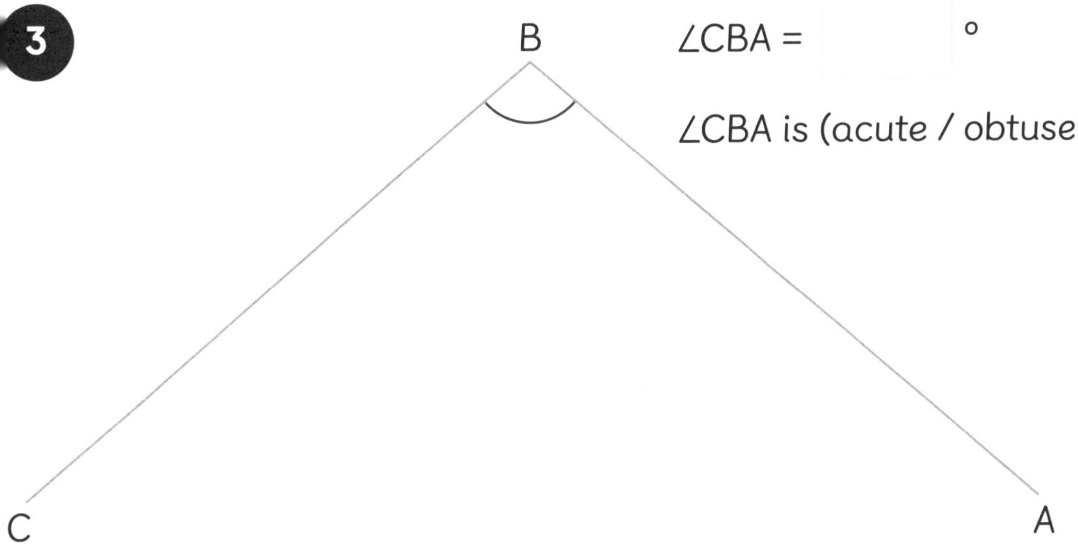

∠CBA = [   ] °

∠CBA is (acute / obtuse / right / straight).

C

A

H

I

J

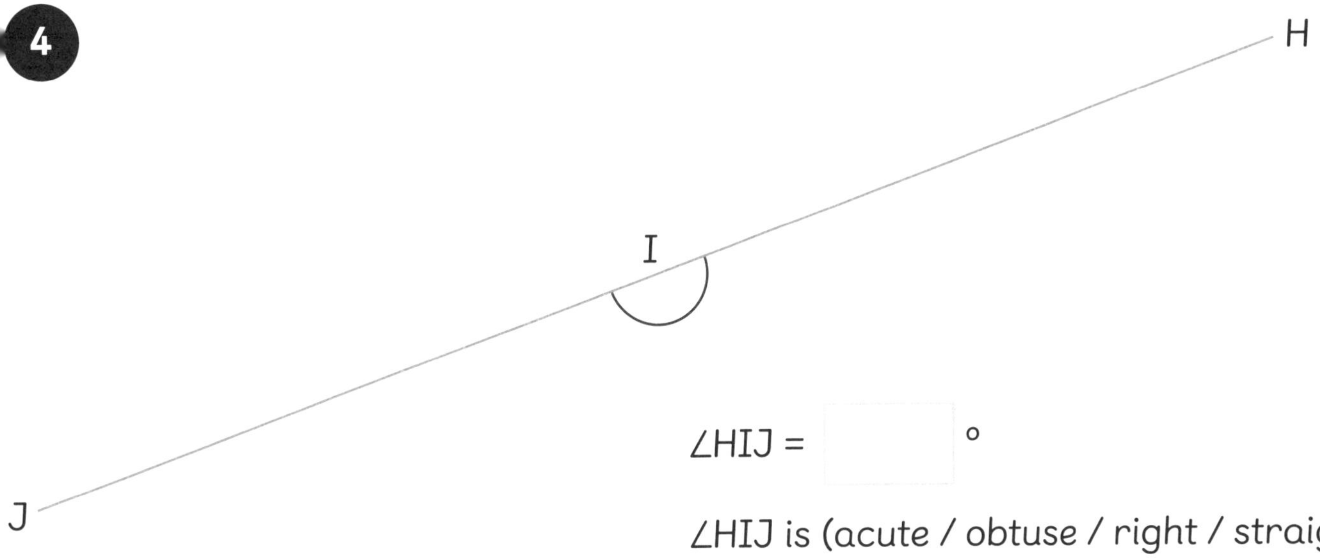

∠HIJ = [   ] °

∠HIJ is (acute / obtuse / right / straight).

U

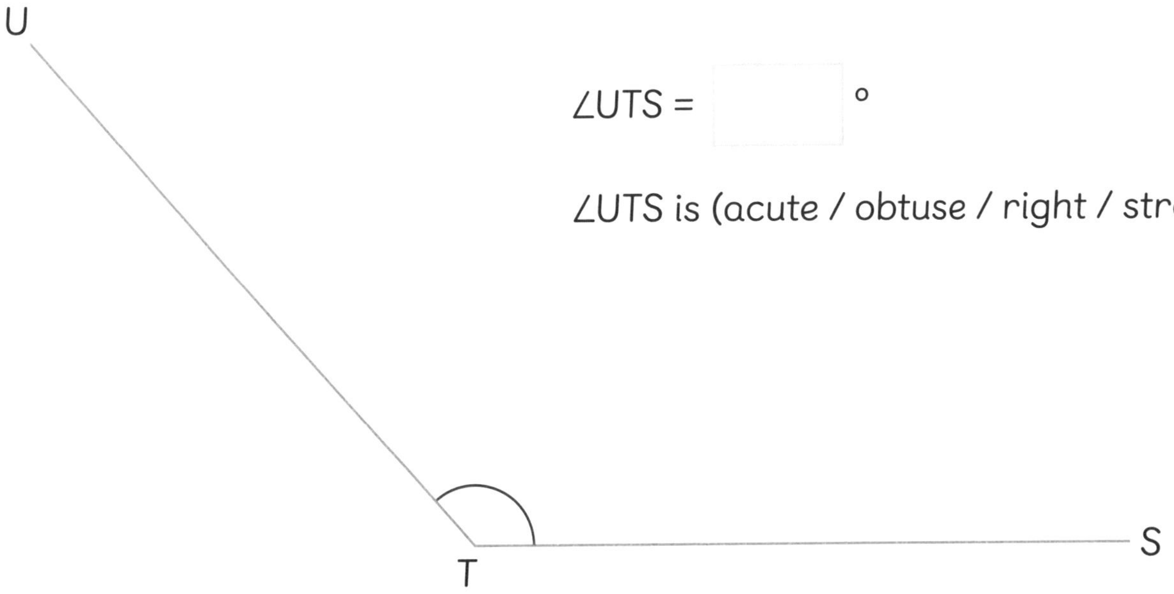

∠UTS = [   ] °

∠UTS is (acute / obtuse / right / straight).

S

T

Drawing angles and lines

Starter

Miss A'liya asked her pupils to draw these figures and answer the following questions.

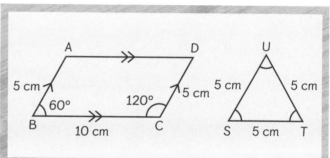

How many degrees is ∠ABC?

How many degrees is ∠ADC?

What is the length of AD?

How many degrees is ∠SUT?

What is the sum of the interior angles of parallelogram ADCB?

What is the sum of the interior angles of the triangle SUT?

Example

We need to use a protractor and a ruler to draw the shapes.

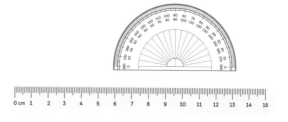

These markings on the lines tell us that each pair of lines are parallel lines.

Let's start with the parallelogram. First, draw the line BC.

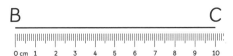

Use the protractor to mark ∠ABC, and then draw the line BA using a ruler.

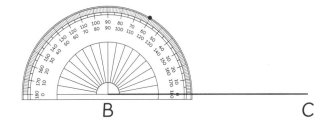

Do the same for ∠BCD. Draw the line CD using a ruler. Then draw the line AD.

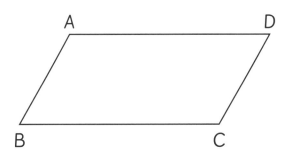

Line AD is the same length as line BC. They are both 10 cm.

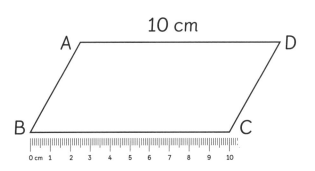

∠ADC is equal to ∠ABC. They are both 60°.

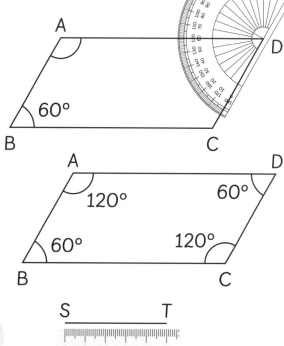

A

60°

B   C

120 + 60 + 120 + 60 = 360
The sum of the interior angles of parallelogram ADCB is 360°.

A   D

120°   60°

60°   120°

B   C

Next, let's draw the triangle. First, draw the line ST.

S   T

0 cm 1   2   3   4   5

Use the protractor to mark ∠UST and then draw the line SU using a ruler.

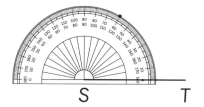

S   T

Do the same for ∠STU and the line TU.

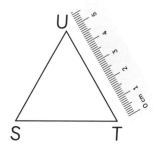

U

S   T

∠SUT is equal to ∠UST and ∠STU. They are all 60°.

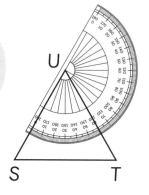

U

S   T

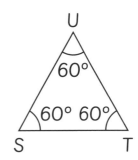

60 + 60 + 60 = 180

The sum of the interior angles of triangle SUT is 180°.

Practice

1 Draw the following shapes using a protractor and a ruler.
Measure the interior angles with a protractor and fill in the blanks.

(a) A square where the length of each side is 120 mm.

The sum of the interior angles is °.

(b) Triangle DEF where EF is 95 mm,
∠DEF is a right angle
and ∠FDE is 60°.

∠EFD is [ ] °.

The sum of the interior angles is [ ] °.

2 Redraw each shape so that the sides are double in length.

(a)

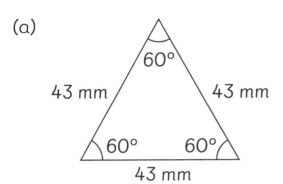

(b)

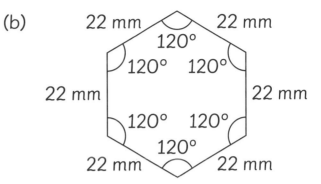

Angles on a straight line

Starter

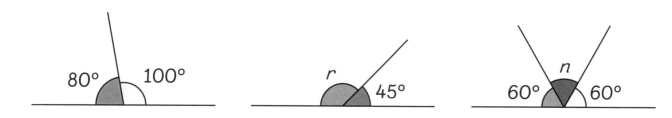

How many degrees are ∠r and ∠n?

Example

When we split a straight line into more than one angle, the sum of the angles is always 180°.

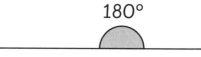

180°

80° 100°

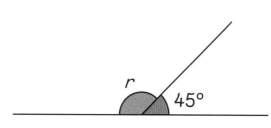

180 − 45 = 135
∠r is 135°.

$$60 + 60 = 120$$
$$180 - 120 = 60$$

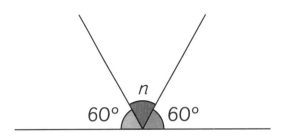

∠r is 135° and ∠n is 60°.

Practice

Find the missing angles and fill in the blanks.

 1

∠t = _____ °

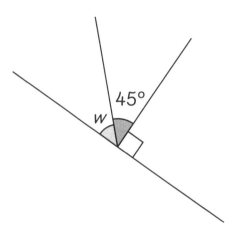 **2**

∠w = _____ °

3

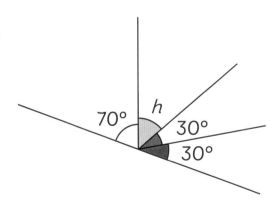

∠h = _____ °

Angles at a point

Starter

Find the size of ∠b and ∠c.
Find the sum of all 3 angles.

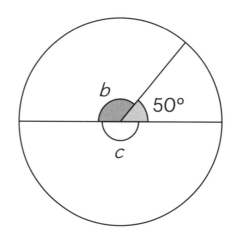

Example

∠b and 50° are
on a straight line.

∠b = 180° – 50°
180 – 50 = 130

Angles on a
straight line = 180°.
∠c = 180°

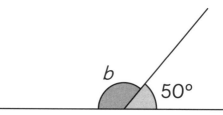

The angles at a point
always add up to 360°.

∠c = 180°
∠b = 130°

The sum of the 3 angles is 360°.

Find the size of each angle and fill in the blanks.

1

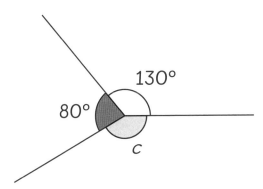

130°

80°

c

∠c =   °

2

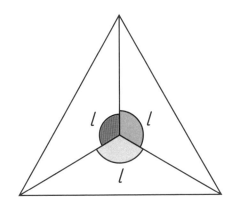

l

l

l

∠l =   °

When we label more than one angle with the same letter it means they are the same size. That letter is called a **variable**.

3

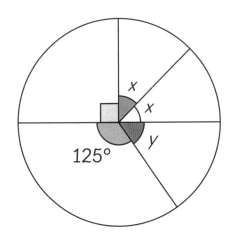

x

x

y

125°

∠x =   °   ∠y =   °

Squares and rectangles

Starter

What do these shapes have in common?

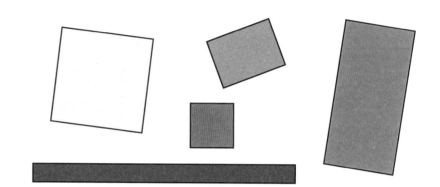

Example

All the shapes have 4 sides. They are all quadrilaterals.

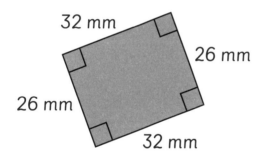
32 mm
26 mm
26 mm
32 mm

All of these quadrilaterals have four 90° angles. That makes them all rectangles.

The opposite sides of rectangles are always the same length.

When 2 lines meet at a 90° angle, we say the lines are perpendicular.

Q   R
P   O

All rectangles have 2 sets of parallel lines. Line QR is parallel to line PO. Line QP is parallel to line RO.

QR is perpendicular to RO and QP. PO is perpendicular to QP and RO.

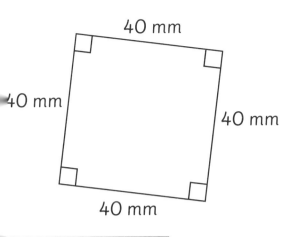

40 mm

40 mm

40 mm

40 mm

Some of the rectangles are also squares. Squares are rectangles with 4 equal length sides.

Practice

DABC is a rectangle.

1 Show which lines are parallel using > and >>.

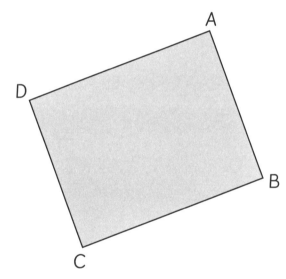

A

D

B

C

2 Fill in the blanks.

(a) Line DA is parallel to line [ ].

(b) Line DC is [ ] to line CB.

(c) Line DC is [ ] to line AB.

(d) ∠ABC is [ ]°.

(e) Line AB is perpendicular to line [ ] and line [ ].

Regular polygons

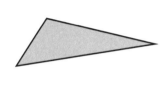 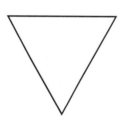  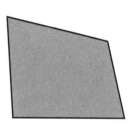

What do these polygons have in common?
What is different about them?

Example

Two of the polygons are triangles.

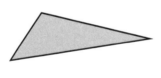 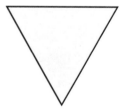

I tore off the corners of the triangles and lined them up at a point.

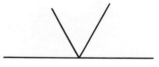

The interior angles of both the triangles add up to 180°.

22

Two of the polygons are quadrilaterals.

Their interior angles add up to 360°.

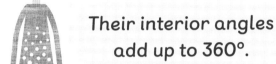

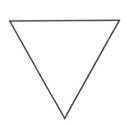

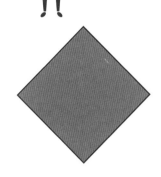

All the sides and angles of this triangle and this rectangle are equal.

When all the sides and angles of a polygon are equal, we say it is a **regular polygon**.

A regular triangle is also called an **equilateral triangle**.

A regular rectangle is also called a **square**.

1   Use a ruler and a protractor to draw a regular rectangle where each side is 73 mm.

2   Use a ruler and a protractor to draw a regular triangle where each side is 85 mm.

3 Circle the shapes that are regular polygons.

4 Draw a regular hexagon where each side is 65 mm and each interior angle is 120°.

Translations

Starter

Describe how to translate
triangle BAC so that
point C ends up at point Y.
What are the coordinates
of points A and B after the
translation?

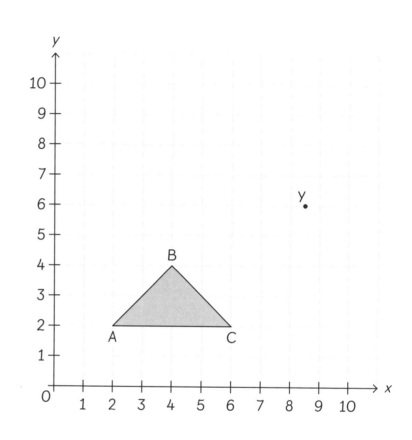

Example

Point C is at (6, 2).

Point Y is at $(8\frac{1}{2}, 6)$.

We need to move point C $2\frac{1}{2}$ units to the right and 4 units up.

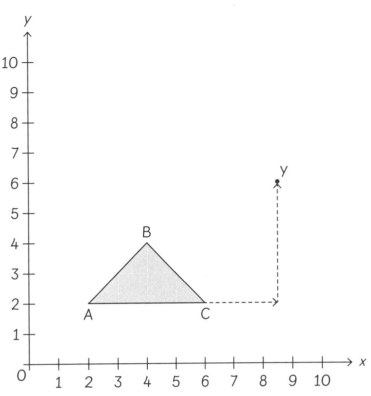

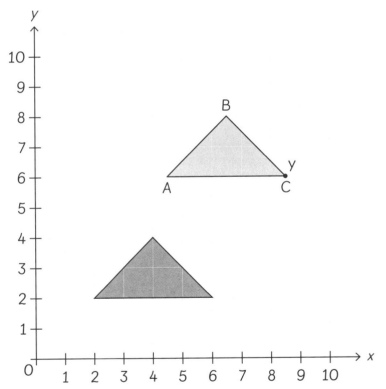

The other points will move by the same amount.

We can look on the grid to find their new positions.

Triangle BAC is translated by $(2\frac{1}{2}, 4)$.

Point A moves from (2, 2) and ends up at $(4\frac{1}{2}, 6)$.

Point B moves from (4, 4) and ends up at $(6\frac{1}{2}, 8)$.

Translate each shape as instructed and draw them on the coordinate grid.

1 F to $(4\frac{1}{2}, 8\frac{1}{2})$

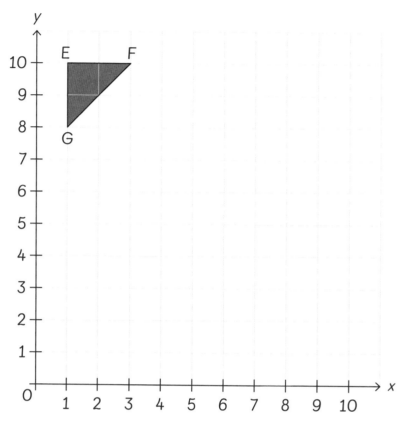

2 J to $(7\frac{1}{2}, 4\frac{1}{2})$

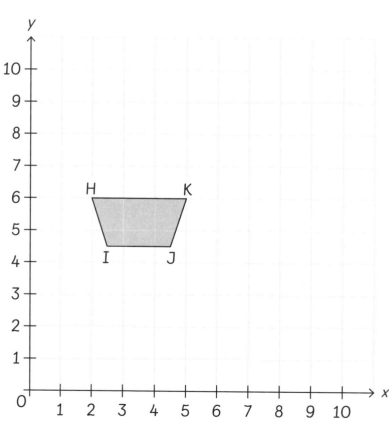

3 P to $(9\frac{1}{2}, 9)$

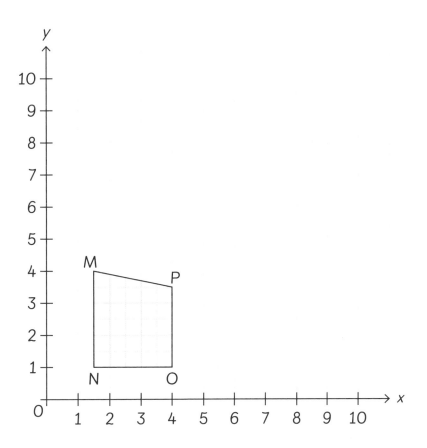

4 T to (6, 1)

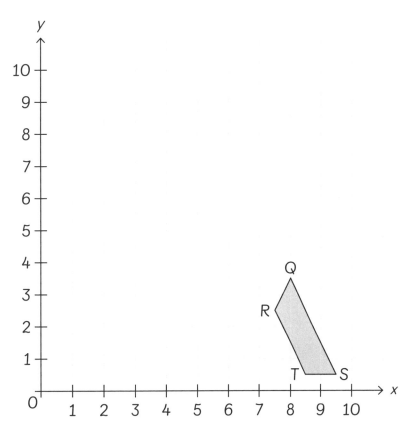

Reflections

Starter

Reflect this image in the horizontal dashed line and then in the vertical dashed line. Draw the shape in its new positions on the grid.

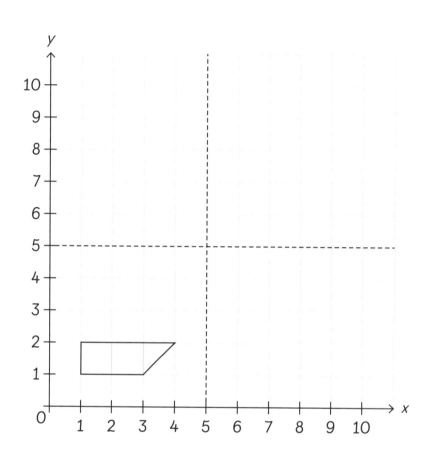

Example

We can call the dashed line the mirror line.

If we were to place a mirror on this line it would show us the reflected image.

First, we need to move each point so that they are the same distance from the horizontal line.

The shape flips over.

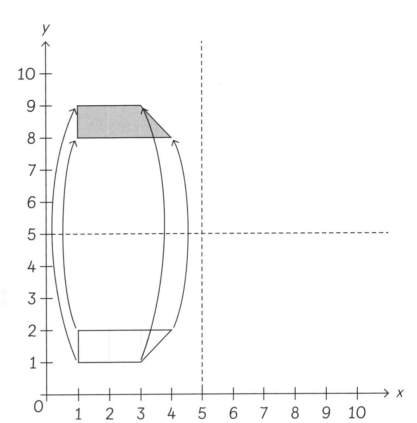

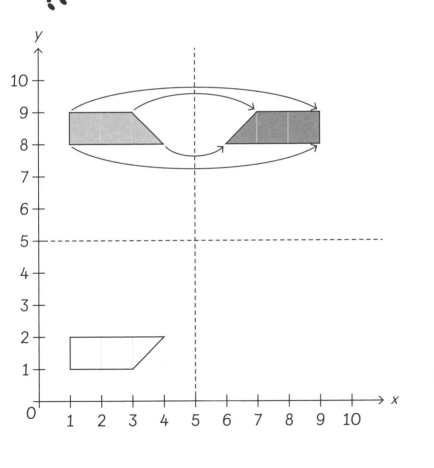

Next, we need to move each point so that they are the same distance from the vertical line.

The shape flips over again.

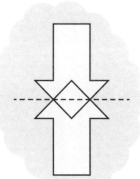

1 Reflect each shape below in the vertical dashed line and then in the horizontal dashed line.

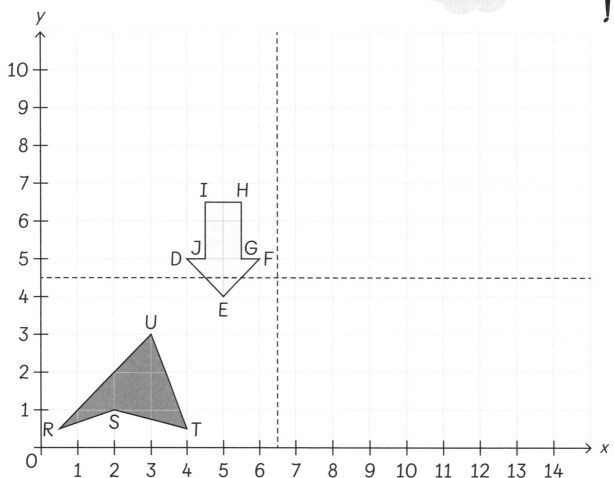

(a) Draw the shapes in their final positions.

(b) Fill in the blanks.

(i) After the two reflections, the coordinates
of vertex S are (⬜ , ⬜).

(ii) After the two reflections, the coordinates
of vertex E are (⬜ , ⬜).

2 The shape below is reflected twice.
It is first reflected in line QR.
It is then reflected in line ST.

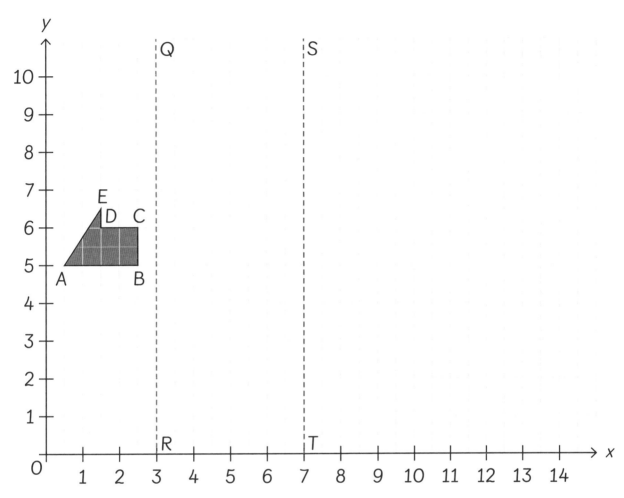

(a) Draw the shape in its final position.

(b) Write the coordinates for the shape in its final position.

Point A = (,   )   Point B = (,   )

Point C = (,   )   Point D = (,   )

Point E = (,   )

Perimeter

Starter

Lulu and Charles want to build a perimeter fence around the school vegetable garden to keep the rabbits out. They draw this plan for the garden.

8 m

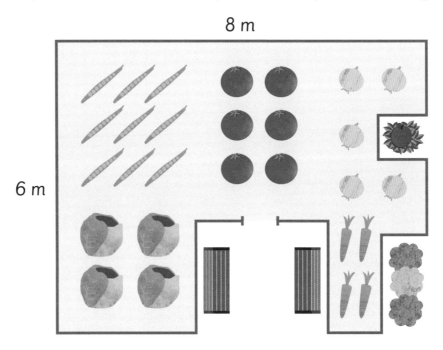

6 m

How many metres of fencing do Lulu and Charles need?

The whole shape fits in a 6 m by 8 m rectangle. If we add the lengths of the sides of the rectangle together, that will tell us how much fencing we need. 6 + 6 + 8 + 8 = 28
We need 28 m of fencing.

I don't think Lulu is correct. I think we need more than 28 m of fencing.

To find out how much fencing Lulu and Charles need, we need to work out the perimeter of the space they want to fence.

Perimeter is the total length of the outside of a shape.

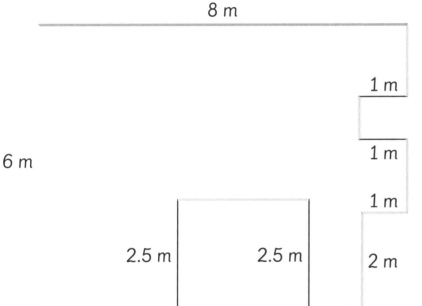

8 m

1 m

1 m

6 m

1 m

2.5 m   2.5 m

2 m

Not all the lengths are shown. We need to work out what some of them are.

The sum of the sides highlighted in pink is equal to the 6 m side highlighted in yellow.

The sum of the sides highlighted in blue is equal to the 8 m side highlighted in green.

We also need to add the sides that are not highlighted.

6 + 6 + 8 + 8 + 2.5 + 2.5 + 1 + 1 = 35

Lulu and Charles need 35 m of fencing for the school vegetable garden.

1 Find the perimeter of the following regular shapes.

(a)

40 mm

[ ] mm

(b)

40 mm

[ ] mm

(c)

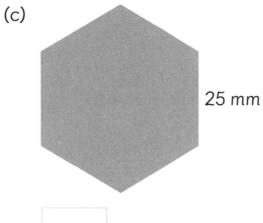

25 mm

[ ] mm

2 Find the perimeter of the following shapes.

(a)

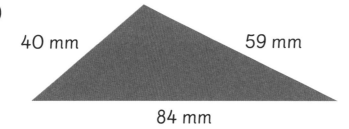

40 mm   59 mm

84 mm

[ ] mm

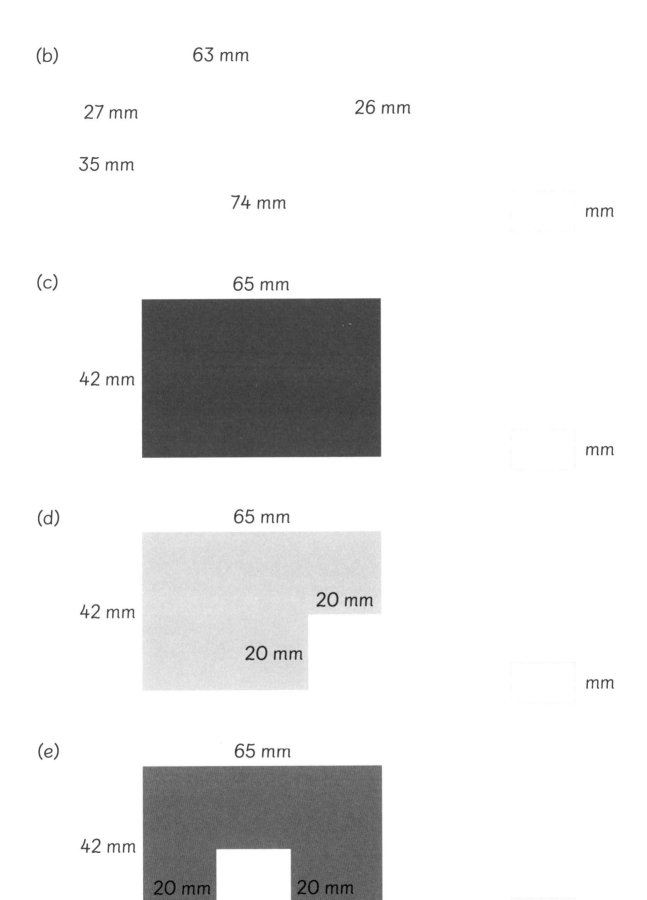

(b)

63 mm

27 mm   26 mm

35 mm

74 mm   ☐ mm

(c)

65 mm

42 mm   ☐ mm

(d)

65 mm

20 mm

42 mm

20 mm   ☐ mm

(e)

65 mm

42 mm

20 mm   20 mm   ☐ mm

Area

Starter

A landscape artist needs to design the entrance to a museum. He draws this plan.

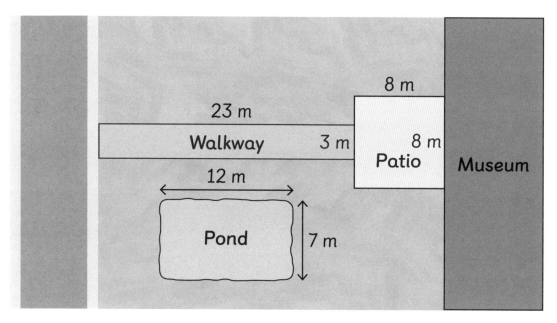

What is the total area of the walkway and the patio?

What is the area of the surface of the pond?

Example

We can measure area in square metres.

A square metre is a square that is 1 m × 1 m.

1 m

1 m

38

The walkway and the patio are both rectangles. We can count the square metres in each rectangle.

We can also multiply to work out how many square metres.

23 m

Walkway 3 m

The walkway is 23 m × 3 m.

23 × 3 = 69
The walkway is 69 square metres.

8 m

Patio 8 m

The patio is 8 m × 8 m.

8 × 8 = 64
The patio is 64 square metres.

We can add the areas to find the total area. 64 + 69 = 133
The total area is 133 square metres.

The pond is a bit tricky because it is not a rectangle, but we can estimate the area.

12 m

Pond 7 m

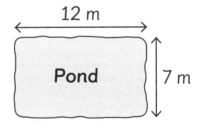

We can write square metres using m².

The pond is approximately 12 m × 7 m.

12 × 7 = 84
It is approximately 84 square metres.

The area of the walkway is 69 m². The area of the patio is 64 m².
The total area of the walkway and the patio is 133 m².

The area of the surface of the pond is approximately 84 m².

1 Find the area of each shape.

(a)

8 cm

5 cm

☐ cm²

(b)

14 cm

7 cm

11 cm

10 cm

4 cm

4 cm

☐ cm²

(c)

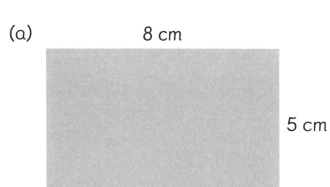

10 cm   10 cm

10 cm   10 cm

☐ cm²

(d)

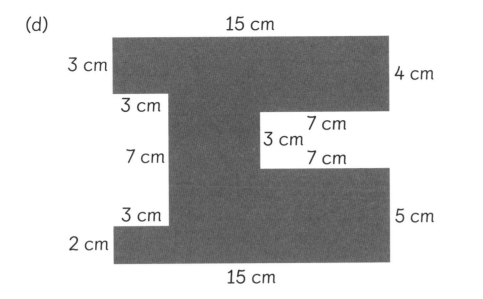

15 cm

3 cm

4 cm

3 cm

7 cm

3 cm

7 cm

7 cm

3 cm

5 cm

2 cm

15 cm

cm²

2 Elliott and his mum want to re-tile the kitchen and bathroom floors. They drew this diagram. The blue area represents the area where they will install new tiles.

How many square metres of new tiles do they need to buy to cover the blue area?

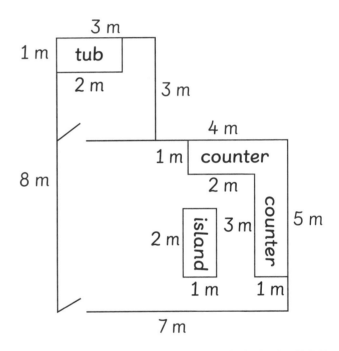

3 m

1 m   tub

2 m

3 m

4 m

1 m   counter

2 m

8 m

2 m   island   3 m   counter   5 m

1 m   1 m

7 m

Elliott and his mum need to buy new tiles to cover an area of ⬜ m².

Review and challenge

1 Label the angles with either reflex, straight, obtuse, right or acute.

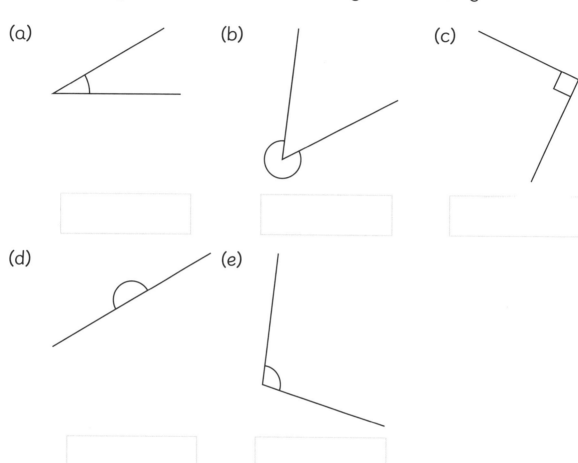

(a)

(b)

(c) ∠UTS is

(d)

(e)

2 Use a protractor to measure ∠UTS.

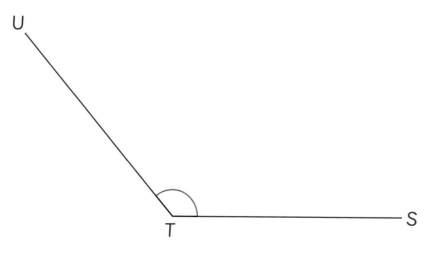

∠UTS is [   ]°.

3 Use a ruler and a protractor to draw the parallelogram as shown in the diagram.

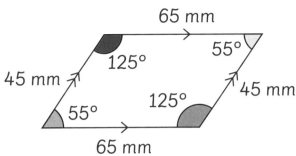

65 mm

45 mm

125°

55°

55°

125°

45 mm

65 mm

4 Use a ruler and a protractor to draw rectangle ABCD so that AB is 62 mm and AD is 43 mm.

AB is parallel to ⬚ . BC is parallel to ⬚ .

AB is perpendicular to ⬚ and ⬚ .

5 Find the missing angles and fill in the blanks.

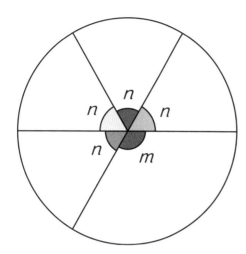

All angles labelled with the same letter are equal.

∠n is ☐ °

∠m is ☐ °

6 Use a ruler and a protractor to draw a regular triangle and a regular rectangle in the space below.

7 Circle the regular polygon.

8 Translate the figure by $(4\frac{1}{2}, 4\frac{1}{2})$ then reflect in the vertical dashed line.

Draw the figure in its new position.

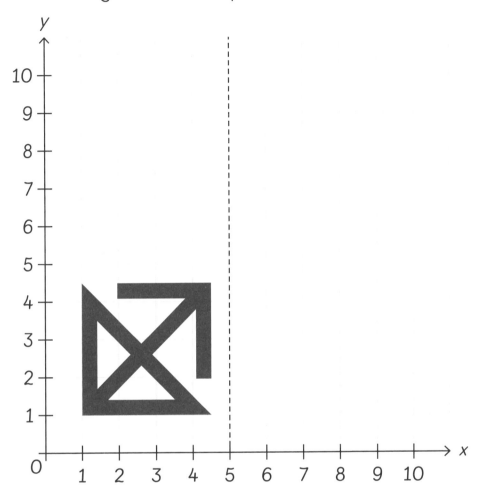

9 Find the area and perimeter for each shape.

(a)

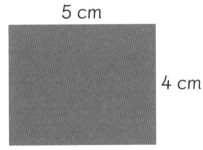

5 cm

4 cm

Perimeter =

Area =

(b)

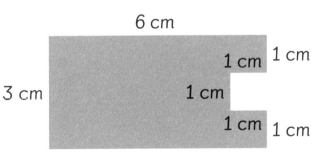

6 cm

1 cm   1 cm

1 cm

1 cm   1 cm

3 cm

Perimeter =

Area =

Answers

Page 5 **1 (a)** Angle *u* is a right angle. **(b)** Angle U is a reflex angle. **(c)** Angle *t* is an obtuse angle. **(d)** Angle *s* is an acute angle. **(e)** There are 4 reflex angles. **(f)** There are 2 right angles. **2 (a)** The interior of a triangle can have up to: 3 acute angles, 1 right angle, 1 obtuse angle. **(b)** The interior of a triangle must have at least 2 acute angles.

Page 8 **1** ∠PQR = 90°. ∠PQR is right. **2** ∠ZYX = 10°. ∠ZYX is acute.

Page 9 **3** ∠CBA = 100°. ∠CBA is obtuse. **4** ∠HIJ = 180°. ∠HIJ is straight. **5** ∠UTS = 132°. ∠UTS is obtuse.

Page 13 **1 (a)**

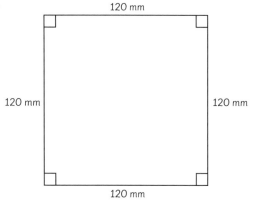

The sum of the interior angles is 360°.

Page 14 **(b)**

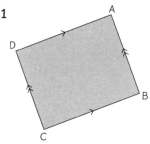

∠EFD is 30°. The sum of the interior angles is 180°.

Page 15 **2 (a)**

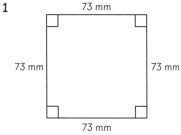

(b)

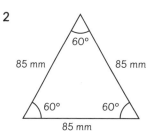

Page 17 **1** ∠*t* = 20° **2** ∠*w* = 45° **3** ∠*h* = 50°

Page 19 **1** ∠*c* = 150° **2** ∠*l* = 120° **3** ∠*x* = 45°, ∠*y* = 55°

Page 21 **1**

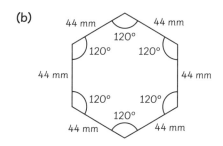

2 (a) Line DA is parallel to line CB. **(b)** Line DC is perpendicular to line CB. **(c)** Line DC is parallel to line AB. **(d)** ∠ABC is 90°. **(e)** Line AB is perpendicular to line DA and line CB.

Page 24 **1** **2**

Page 25 **3**

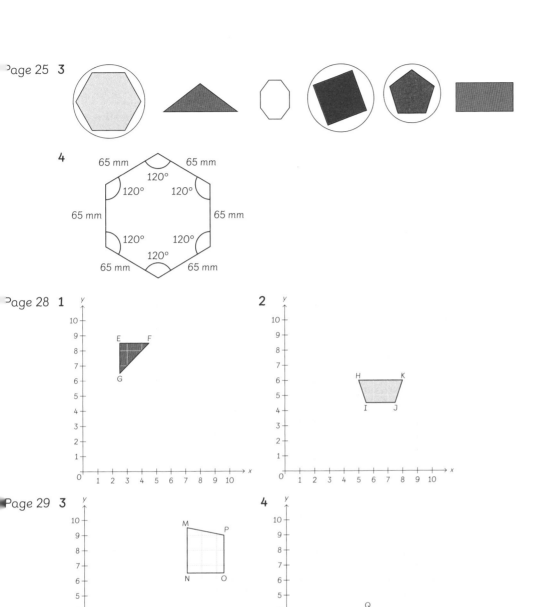

4

Page 28 **1**   **2**

Page 29 **3**   **4**

Page 32 **1 (a)**

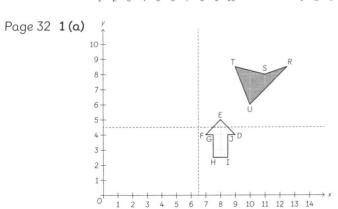

(b) (i) After the two reflections, the coordinates of vertex S are (11, 8). **(ii)** After the two reflections, the coordinates of vertex E are (8, 5).

Answers continued

Page 33 **2 (a)**

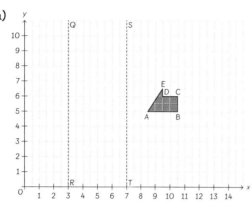

(b) Point A = $(8\frac{1}{2}, 5)$; Point B = $(10\frac{1}{2}, 5)$; Point C = $(10\frac{1}{2}, 6)$;

Point D = $(9\frac{1}{2}, 6)$; Point E = $(9\frac{1}{2}, 6\frac{1}{2})$

Page 36 **1 (a)** 120 mm **(b)** 160 mm **(c)** 150 mm **2 (a)** 40 + 59 + 84 = 183; 183 mm

Page 37 **(b)** 27 + 63 + 26 + 74 + 35 = 225; 225 mm **(c)** 42 + 65 + 42 + 65 = 214; 214 mm
(d) 42 + 65 + 22 + 20 + 20 + 45 = 214 OR 42 + 65 + 42 + 65 = 214; 214 mm **(e)** 42 + 65 + 42 + 20 + 20 + 65 = 254; 254 mm

Page 40 **1 (a)** 40 cm² **(b)** 114 cm² **(c)** 100 cm²

Page 41 **(d)** 138 cm² **2** Elliott and his mum need to buy new tiles to cover an area of 34 m².

Page 42 **1 (a)** acute **(b)** reflex **(c)** right **(d)** straight **(e)** obtuse **2** ∠UTS is 130°.

Page 43 **3**

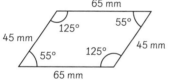

4

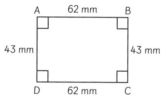

AB is parallel to DC. BC is parallel to AD.
AB is perpendicular to AD and BC.

Page 44 **5** ∠n is 60°. ∠m is 120°.
6 Answers may vary. For example:

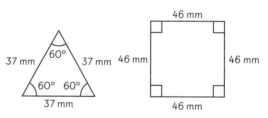

7

Page 45 **8**

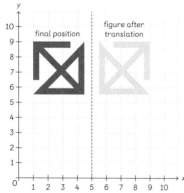

9 (a) Perimeter = 18 cm; Area = 20 cm²
(b) Perimeter = 20 cm; Area = 17 cm²